Vocabulary Tests
Level 2

Suitable for ages 8 – 10

Each word study unit contains

- Definition matching
- Cloze sentences

Contents

Unit 1	page 2
Unit 2	page 4
Unit 3	page 6
Unit 4	page 8
Unit 5	page 10
Unit 6	page 12
Unit 7	page 14
Unit 8	page 16
Unit 9	page 18
Unit 10	page 20
Test 1	page 22
Test 2	page 26
Test 3	page 30
Test 4	page 34
Test 5	page 38

Solutions

Unit 1	page 42
Unit 2	page 42
Unit 3	page 42
Unit 4	page 43
Unit 5	page 43
Unit 6	page 44
Unit 7	page 44
Unit 8	page 44
Unit 9	page 45
Unit 10	page 45
Test 1	page 46
Test 2	page 47
Test 3	page 48
Test 4	page 49
Test 5	page 50

Copyright © 2017 Simon Steggels
All rights reserved

No part of this book may be reproduced, stored in a retrieval system, communicated or transmitted in any form or by any means without prior written permission. All inquiries should be made to the publisher.

ISBN 978-0-6480967-6-4

Published by
Advanced Instruction Pty Ltd
www.advancedinstruction.com.au

Unit 1

Definitions—match the words in the bold with their meanings below

surface	tennis	marsh	lava
breath	gum tree	trudged	equipment
polar	branches	sobbing	pouring
Arctic	nest	frantically	scientists

1. walked with a lot of effort over a difficult surface _____
2. in a way that is nearly out of control because of strong emotion _____
3. the top layer of something _____
4. a structure built by birds or insects to leave their eggs in _____
5. the air that goes into and out of the lungs _____
6. the ground near a lake, a river, or the sea that is always wet _____
7. relating to the North or South Pole or the areas around them _____
8. parts of a tree that grow out from the main trunk and have leaves, flowers, or fruit on them _____
9. eucalyptus _____
10. the very cold area around the North Pole _____
11. flowing quickly and in large amounts _____
12. the set of tools needed for a particular purpose _____
13. experts who study or work in one of the sciences _____
14. hot liquid rock that comes out of the Earth through a volcano _____
15. crying noisily while taking in deep breaths _____
16. a game played between two or four people that involves hitting a small ball across a net using a racket _____

Unit 1

Word usage—complete the sentences using the words in bold from the previous page

1. The _____ were busy doing experiments on the volcano.

2. The old bus was _____ out thick, black exhaust fumes.

3. Some of the sport _____ is damaged and must be replaced.

4. Molten _____ flowed down the side of the volcano.

5. As the helicopter flew overhead, we waved _____, trying to attract the pilot's attention.

6. I had to stop running to catch my _____.

7. After our long walk in the rain, we _____ back toward the house.

8. I found my sister _____ because she'd broken her favourite doll.

9. At the mouth of the river is a large area of _____ land.

10. _____ bears live only in the Arctic region.

11. Neil Armstrong was the first person to walk on the _____ of the moon.

12. You will find a koala bear in a _____, eating eucalyptus leaves.

13. The North Pole is located in the middle of the _____ Ocean.

14. The fruit on the lower _____ was protected from the sun.

15. Cuckoos are famous for laying their eggs in the _____ of another bird.

16. My friend and I played two games of _____ yesterday.

© MR STEGGELS ADVANCED INSTRUCTION PTY LTD

Unit 2

Definitions—match the words in the bold with their meanings below

action-packed	practice	shudder	game park
adventure	sideways	floundered	misspent
blockbuster	enemies	despite	crops
produced	forehead	crooked	rangers

1. in a direction to the left or right, not forwards or backwards _____
2. a book or film that is very successful _____
3. full of exciting events _____
4. experienced great difficulties or was totally unable to decide what to do or say next _____
5. created something _____
6. to shake suddenly because of a very unpleasant feeling _____
7. without taking any notice of _____
8. not forming a straight line, or having many bends _____
9. an unusual, exciting trip or experience _____
10. money or time that is wasted _____
11. something that is usually or regularly done _____
12. grains, fruits or vegetables grown in large amounts _____
13. people whose job is to protect a forest or natural park _____
14. an area of land set aside to protect wild animals _____
15. the flat part of the face, above the eyes and below the hair _____
16. people who hate each other _____

Unit 2

Word usage—complete the sentences using the words in bold from the previous page

1. The forest _____ help to keep animals safe from hunters and poachers.

2. The main _____ grown for export are coffee and rice.

3. We must stop public money being _____ in this way.

4. Many tourists visited the _____ to see wild animals in their habitat.

5. Our cat _____ four kittens last night.

6. It was an _____ weekend of skiing and mountain biking.

7. *Triassic World* is a _____ movie that has earned a lot of money.

8. If you move _____ to the left, I can get everyone in the picture.

9. He won't come rock climbing; he has no sense of _____.

10. I still enjoyed camp _____ the cold and rainy weather.

11. Max stole Lee's pocket money and they've been _____ ever since.

12. He lost the next page of his speech and _____ for a few seconds.

13. I heard a massive explosion and the ground _____ beneath me.

14. She has a scar on her _____ from when she fell off the slippery dip.

15. I need to get some more _____ before I take my driving test.

16. You must drive slowly on these _____ country roads.

© MR STEGGELS ADVANCED INSTRUCTION PTY LTD

Unit 3

Definitions—match the words in the bold with their meanings below

maid	elders	jersey	information
master	carrier	grueling	connected
old-fashioned	billabong	network	Internet
soot	plains	sabotage	website

1. belonging to a time in the past
2. a servant
3. large areas of flat land
4. older people especially with respected positions in society
5. to destroy equipment, weapons, or buildings on purpose
6. a number of computers that are connected together
7. a person who employs servants; a dog's owner
8. facts about a situation, person or event
9. a low area of ground that that fills up during a flood
10. a person or thing that holds or transports something
11. joined together
12. a shirt that is worn by a member of a sports team
13. a set of pages on the Internet about a particular subject
14. the world-wide system of connected computers that allows people to share information and communicate
15. extremely tiring and difficult, needing great effort
16. a black powder produced when coal or wood are burned

Unit 3

Word usage—complete the sentences using the words in bold from the previous page

1. For more information about the courses we offer, visit our _____.

2. This football _____ is made from 100 percent cotton.

3. I learned about volcanoes by researching for information on the _____.

4. I eventually won the grand final after five _____ sets.

5. High mountains rise above the western _____.

6. With careful training, a dog will obey its _____.

7. Our TV won't work if the aerial is not _____ properly.

8. At the beach resort, the apartments and villas have a daily _____ service.

9. We set up camp by a _____, under the shade of a large tree.

10. If you want to succeed, you should listen to the advice of your _____.

11. The farmer relied on a water _____ to fill his tank in times of drought.

12. The opposing team tried to _____ our bikes by slashing the tyres.

13. My aunty bought me a very _____ looking cardigan.

14. The flyer gave a phone number that could be used to get more _____.

15. The company spent $1.8 million to improve their computer _____.

16. It is dangerous to let too much _____ build up inside a chimney.

© MR STEGGELS ADVANCED INSTRUCTION PTY LTD

Unit 4

Definitions—match the words in the bold with their meanings below

lightning	**grouch**	**punished**	**computer**
beanie	**dangerous**	**tales**	**animated**
headlights	**nerves**	**squash**	**production**
umbrella	**neighbourhood**	**revolting**	**complex**

1. a hat made from wool with a small round ball on top _____
2. disgusting, especially in taste _____
3. light produced by electricity moving between clouds or from clouds to the ground _____
4. stories about imaginary events or people _____
5. someone who complains a lot or is often angry _____
6. a game played in a special closed area that involves hitting a small rubber ball against a wall _____
7. the two lights on the front of a car used for driving at night _____
8. the area surrounding your home _____
9. a worried feeling when you feel you might fail _____
10. likely to harm, damage or kill _____
11. an electronic device that stores information and runs programs _____
12. gave a penalty to _____
13. describes films, drawings and models that are filmed in a way that makes them appear to move _____
14. a show put on for an audience _____
15. a device for protection against the rain _____
16. difficult to understand _____

© MR STEGGELS ADVANCED INSTRUCTION PTY LTD

Unit 4

Word usage—complete the sentences using the words in bold from the previous page

1. The storyteller shared some exciting _____ with the children.

2. My _____ is full of kids riding bikes and dogs barking.

3. My supervisor is a real _____; she is always in a bad mood.

4. A case of _____ won't stop me from performing tonight.

5. I had to wear a _____ to protect my head from the cold.

6. Those responsible for burning down our school must be _____.

7. On the road up ahead, I saw a car's _____ coming towards me.

8. The tree in our backyard was struck by _____ and fell over.

9. My parents won't let me play ice hockey because they think it's too _____.

10. The girl left her _____ on the bus yesterday.

11. My little brother cooked a banana and broccoli cake; it tasted _____.

12. The plot of that book is so _____ that I can't understand it.

13. Our school put on a _____ of a musical called *The Flying Carpet*.

14. Many films created for children are _____.

15. The hard drive of my _____ was full so I needed to back up my files.

16. We hired a _____ court at our local gym.

© MR STEGGELS ADVANCED INSTRUCTION PTY LTD

Unit 5

Definitions—match the words in the bold with their meanings below

particular	**linked**	**extinct**	**health**
arteries	**spiritual**	**mythical**	**habits**
veins	**self-defence**	**isolated**	**illness**
waste	**overcome**	**recorded**	**medicine**

1. no longer existing _____

2. this one and not any other _____

3. to defeat an opponent or conquer a fear _____

4. connected to _____

5. the skill of fighting without weapons to protect yourself _____

6. imaginary or not real _____

7. tubes that carry blood to the heart from other parts of the body _____

8. alone or apart from others _____

9. not physical; relating to religious beliefs _____

10. a measure of how free from illness you are _____

11. captured a performance using electronic equipment _____

12. what is left after useful parts have been removed _____

13. regular practices that are sometimes hard to give up _____

14. tubes that carry blood from the heart to other parts of the body _____

15. the state of being sick _____

16. a substance, especially in the form of a liquid or a pill, used to treat illness or injury _____

© MR STEGGELS ADVANCED INSTRUCTION PTY LTD

Unit 5

Word usage—complete the sentences using the words in bold from the previous page

1. The doctor told me to take two spoonfuls of _____ with breakfast.

2. She had five days off work due to _____.

3. I was taught to drive by my father so I've picked up some of his bad _____.

4. Regular exercise is good for your _____.

5. The child wouldn't take just any book - he had to have this _____ one!

6. My favourite film features dragons and other _____ creatures.

7. _____ carry blood to the heart.

8. A high, stone wall _____ the house from the rest of the village.

9. Hardening of the _____ can lead to a heart attack.

10. My grandmother listens to _____ music sung by church choirs.

11. My sister goes to _____ classes to learn martial arts.

12. Eventually the girl managed to _____ her shyness in class.

13. The two explosions are not thought to be _____ in any way.

14. The kidneys and liver are vital in getting rid of _____ from the body.

15. The dodo bird went _____ shortly after it came into contact with humans.

16. The camera man _____ their wedding on his video camera.

© MR STEGGELS ADVANCED INSTRUCTION PTY LTD

Unit 6

Definitions—match the words in the bold with their meanings below

puzzled	BMX	urge	between
aching	missiles	anxiously	obey
lawn	advertising	quite	undercurrent
gleefully	shoplift	too	rip

1. in addition, also _____
2. an area of grass, especially near to a house or in a park, that is cut regularly to keep it short _____
3. in a way that shows you are worried and nervous _____
4. continuous unpleasant pain _____
5. to take goods illegally from a store without paying _____
6. in a way that shows happiness, excitement, or pleasure _____
7. into, at or across the space separating two things _____
8. confused because you do not understand something _____
9. the activity of producing messages about products and services that persuade people to buy _____
10. a current below the surface _____
11. a strong wish, especially one that is difficult to control _____
12. to behave according to a rule _____
13. to a certain degree _____
14. flying weapons that can travel a long distance _____
15. a narrow current of water strongest near the surface that pulls away from the shore _____
16. bicycle motocross; stunt riding over an obstacle course _____

Unit 6

Word usage—complete the sentences using the words in bold from the previous page

1. My brother races his _____ bike at the track each weekend.

2. A _____ can occur at any beach where there are breaking waves.

3. It is illegal to _____ items from a store.

4. My mother creates colourful _____ posters for her cupcake shop.

5. My teacher had a _____ look on his face when he saw my answer.

6. I've got _____ muscles after the cross-country run yesterday.

7. Some of the soldiers refused to _____ orders.

8. Stones, bottles, and other _____ were thrown by the protestors.

9. We are going to *Wild 'n Wet Water Park*. Would you like to come _____?

10. The competitors waited _____ outside the stadium before their race.

11. Someone needs to mow our front _____ as the grass is knee-high!

12. I had a sudden _____ to go for a walk in the fresh air.

13. The children ran down the stairs _____ on Christmas morning.

14. The boys have been working on their project for _____ some time.

15. The children's mother insisted that they swim _____ the flags at the beach.

16. I could feel the strong _____ when I dived to the bottom of the river.

© MR STEGGELS ADVANCED INSTRUCTION PTY LTD

Unit 7

Definitions—match the words in the bold with their meanings below

cute	proud	dawdle	fashion
apes	thread	moaned	flared
disaster	tramp	furious	business
clump	bronze	neat	baggy

1. a style that is popular at a particular time _____
2. extremely angry _____
3. pleasant and attractive especially a puppy, kitten or a baby _____
4. made a long, low sound of pain _____
5. a brown metal made of copper and tin _____
6. animals like large monkeys with no tail, that use their arms to move through trees _____
7. to walk, especially long distances or with heavy steps _____
8. a group or solid mass of something _____
9. very good, excellent; tidy, well-presented _____
10. an event that results in great harm, damage, or death _____
11. very happy with your own achievements or the achievements of someone you are close to _____
12. becoming wider at one end _____
13. loose-fitting clothing _____
14. the activity of buying and selling goods and services _____
15. to walk very slowly _____
16. a long, thin strand of cotton used in sewing _____

Unit 7

Word usage—complete the sentences using the words in bold from the previous page

1. Now that I have lost weight, my clothes are _____ on me.

2. Our company does a lot of _____ with overseas customers.

3. My friend's baby brother is really _____ when he smiles.

4. My friend will often _____ on the way to school and arrive late to class.

5. The church bells are made of _____.

6. Chimpanzees and gorillas are examples of _____.

7. My parents were _____ when I won first place in a writing competition.

8. _____ trousers are no longer in fashion; people like straight leg pants.

9. The injured man _____ with pain before losing consciousness.

10. I worked with a needle and _____ to repair my socks.

11. There was a big _____ of soil on the farmer's boots.

12. I was late for work again and my boss was _____ with me.

13. Everything was going smoothly at the skydiving show until _____ struck.

14. The children had to _____ through the woods to reach the campsite.

15. My brother's new 3D video game is really _____.

16. My sister spends most of her money on _____.

© MR STEGGELS ADVANCED INSTRUCTION PTY LTD

Unit 8

Definitions—match the words in the bold with their meanings below

scurried	ragged	rugby	satisfied
antennae	folktale	crowding	boomerang
colony	barn	possibly	example
trousers	hopeful	confidence	reporter

1. a sport where two teams try to score points by carrying a ball across a particular line _____

2. a pair of long, thin organs that are found on the heads of insects and crustaceans _____

3. contented, pleased _____

4. clothing that is torn and not in good condition _____

5. gathering in a group around someone or something _____

6. a large building on a farm in which animals are kept _____

7. moved quickly, with small, short steps _____

8. being certain of your abilities or having trust in people _____

9. feeling positive about a future event _____

10. perhaps, likely, maybe _____

11. a piece of clothing worn on the lower part of the body with two cylinder-shaped parts, one for each leg _____

12. a curved stick that returns to the person who threw it _____

13. a person whose job is to discover information about news events and present them in a newspaper, on radio or TV _____

14. something that is typical of a group of things _____

15. a group of animals or plants of the same type that live together _____

16. a traditional story that people of a particular region or group repeat among themselves _____

Unit 8

Word usage—complete the sentences using the words in bold from the previous page

1. Aboriginal people used the _____ as a hunting weapon.

2. My father needs a pair of _____ to match his new jacket.

3. I worked as a _____ for Channel 13 News and Current Affairs.

4. The tutor asked Trevor to give an _____ of a fairy tale.

5. Ants use their _____ to communicate with each other.

6. The farmer keeps his horses in the _____ along with the hay and feed.

7. The cat _____ after the mouse as it raced toward the hole in the floor.

8. My friend has the _____ to talk calmly in front of the entire school.

9. *Cinderella* is a _____ written by Jacob and Wilhelm Grimm.

10. The children were _____ that their teacher would let them play cards.

11. When I work in the garden, I wear dirty, _____ clothes.

12. His coach was not _____ with his average performance last game.

13. A _____ of ants had made its home in our living room wall.

14. People were _____ around the limousine, hoping to catch a glimpse of their favourite pop singer.

15. We could _____ make the grand final, if we win by 15 or more goals.

16. My brother plays _____ every Saturday morning.

© MR STEGGELS ADVANCED INSTRUCTION PTY LTD

Unit 9

Definitions—match the words in the bold with their meanings below

polite	brilliant	suggest	throughout
seriously	meant	judge	assortment
media	translate	panic	transform
welcoming	adequate	temporary	everlasting

1. to decide right from wrong
2. TV, newspapers, radio etc. as a group
3. well-mannered
4. change written or spoken words into a different language
5. on purpose, intended to make something happen
6. very bright in colour or light, or very clever
7. greeting someone in a friendly, polite way
8. not in a joking manner
9. enough
10. to put forward an idea or plan for others to consider
11. uncontrollable fear causing wild behaviour
12. lasting only for a limited time
13. to completely change the appearance of
14. in every part of a place or object
15. permanent, never ending
16. a mixture of different kinds of things

© MR STEGGELS ADVANCED INSTRUCTION PTY LTD

Unit 9

Word usage—complete the sentences using the words in bold from the previous page

1. Every morning, on the island, we were greeted by _____ sunshine.

2. I was asked to _____ the art competition.

3. The council plans to _____ the rubbish dump into a beautiful park.

4. We were not given _____ time to prepare our speeches.

5. We don't have an _____ supply of water, so please use it wisely.

6. We came away from the farmer's market with an _____ of vegetables.

7. If you don't think my plan is good, can you _____ another one?

8. I managed to get myself a _____ job over the Christmas holiday period.

9. The author needed someone to _____ her book into Mandarin.

10. Members of the _____ were not allowed in the courtroom for the trial.

11. The hotel manager was _____ and showed me to my room.

12. He was _____ injured when he fell off his motorbike at high speed.

13. It is not _____ to put your feet on the table.

14. The heavy rain continued to fall _____ the day.

15. I _____ to remind you to take your assignment to school today.

16. People began to _____ when they saw the flames in the doorway.

Unit 10

Definitions—match the words in the bold with their meanings below

overhanging	magician	naughtiest	professor
shore	handkerchief	sighed	supersonic
cooed	squawk	hospital	combustion
perched	cheeky	cabbage	hydrogen

1. the land along the edge of a sea, lake, or wide river _____
2. slightly rude or showing no respect, but often in a funny way _____
3. a place where people who are ill or injured are treated _____
4. made a low soft sound _____
5. sticking out over something at a lower level _____
6. breathed out slowly and noisily, expressing tiredness _____
7. sat on or near the edge of something, especially a bird _____
8. a square piece of cloth or paper used for cleaning the nose _____
9. worst behaved _____
10. the lightest gas, with no colour, taste, or smell, and combines with oxygen to form water _____
11. a teacher at university _____
12. a person who has magic powers in stories, or who performs tricks for entertainment _____
13. burning _____
14. a large round vegetable with green, white, or purple leaves that can be eaten cooked or uncooked _____
15. faster than the speed of sound _____
16. to make an unpleasantly loud, sharp cry _____

Unit 10

Word usage—complete the sentences using the words in bold from the previous page

1. My younger brother has a _____ grin.

2. The tiny village is _____ on top of a high hill.

3. Several large trees were _____ the path.

4. Our boat was a long way from _____ when the engine died.

5. Water is made up of two elements: _____ and oxygen.

6. The pigeon sat outside my window and _____ softly.

7. The _____ student in class threw her books on the floor.

8. 'I'll never understand fractions,' the boy _____.

9. My father took out his _____ and blew his nose loudly.

10. The sprinter had to go into _____ to have an operation on her foot.

11. Stephen Hawking is probably the most famous _____ in the world.

12. If the fox comes into the yard, the chickens will _____.

13. My mother is cooking _____ soup for dinner—yuck!

14. _____ gives off heat, light and smoke.

15. My brother's dream is to fly a _____ fighter plane.

16. Merlin is a _____ in the stories of King Arthur and the Knights of the Round Table.

© MR STEGGELS ADVANCED INSTRUCTION PTY LTD

Test 1

1. Which word means **flowing quickly and in large amounts**?

   A molten
   B frantically
   C sobbing
   D pouring

2. Choose the best meaning of the word **adventure**

   A in a way that is nearly out of control because of strong emotion
   B a book or film that is very successful
   C an unusual, exciting trip or experience
   D facts about a situation, person or event

3. Choose the word that is closest in meaning to **wreck**

   A sabotage
   B grueling
   C dangerous
   D squash

4. Choose the word that is most opposite in meaning to **rewarded**

   A recorded
   B puzzled
   C shuddered
   D punished

5. Which is the odd word out?

   A arteries
   B veins
   C forehead
   D health

© MR STEGGELS ADVANCED INSTRUCTION PTY LTD

6. Choose the word that best completes the sentence

   To learn about lions, I searched for _____ on the Internet.

   A   example
   B   information
   C   website
   D   tales

7. The letters in **delser** can be rearranged to make a word meaning

   A   older people especially with respected positions in society
   B   large areas of flat land
   C   extremely tiring and difficult, needing great effort
   D   the area surrounding your home

8. Which pair of words is closest in meaning?

   A   illness   medicine
   B   complex   dangerous
   C   mythical   spiritual
   D   connected   linked

9. Which pair of words is most opposite in meaning?

   A   obey   naughtiest
   B   frantically anxiously
   C   temporary   everlasting
   D   quite   too

10. Which word should replace the words in bold in the following sentence?

    The criminal had to **completely change** his appearance to avoid being captured.

    A   judge
    B   translate
    C   transform
    D   suggest

© MR STEGGELS ADVANCED INSTRUCTION PTY LTD

11. Which prefix must be added to the word **spent** to make its opposite?

    A   ill-
    B   im-
    C   mis-
    D   dis-

12. What do the letters **BMX** stand for?

    A   bicycle motor cross
    B   bicycle motocross
    C   bicycle moves extreme
    D   bicycles moto extreme

13. Which word means **to a certain degree**?

    A   quite
    B   seriously
    C   possibly
    D   example

14. Choose the word that is most similar in meaning to **confused**

    A   satisfied
    B   puzzled
    C   welcoming
    D   isolated

15. Which is the odd word out?

    A   professor
    B   magician
    C   reporter
    D   advertising

© MR STEGGELS ADVANCED INSTRUCTION PTY LTD

16. Choose the word that best completes the sentence

    Martial arts is a form of _____.

    A   health
    B   medicine
    C   self-defence
    D   practice

---

17. The letters in **ginahc** can be rearranged to make a word meaning

    A   continuous unpleasant pain
    B   in a way that shows happiness, excitement, or pleasure
    C   extremely angry
    D   a style that is popular at a particular time

---

18. Which pair of words is closest in meaning?

    A   tramp   dawdle
    B   headlights lightning
    C   baggy   neat
    D   proud   furious

---

19. Choose the best definition of the word **computer**

    A   the world-wide system of devices that allows users to share information
    B   an electronic device that stores information and runs programs
    C   a set of pages on the Internet about a particular subject
    D   films, drawings, models that are shown in a way that makes them move

---

20. Which word should replace the words in bold in the following sentence?

    The questions in the test were too **difficult to understand** for students in the first grade.

    A   crooked
    B   grueling
    C   complex
    D   hopeful

© MR STEGGELS ADVANCED INSTRUCTION PTY LTD

Test 2

1. Which word means **to make an unpleasantly loud, sharp cry**?

    A   squawk
    B   cooed
    C   sighed
    D   moan

2. Choose the best meaning of the word **perched**

    A   sticking out over something at a lower level
    B   gathering in a group around someone or something
    C   in every part of a place or object
    D   sat on or near the edge of something

3. Choose the word that is closest in meaning to **contented**

    A   cheeky
    B   hopeful
    C   animated
    D   satisfied

4. Choose the word that is most opposite in meaning to **illness**

    A   nerves
    B   breath
    C   health
    D   extinct

5. Which is the odd word out?

    A   gleefully
    B   seriously
    C   hopeful
    D   anxiously

© MR STEGGELS ADVANCED INSTRUCTION PTY LTD

6. Choose the word that best completes the sentence

   On our zoo excursion, we had _____ time to see all of the animals.

   A   adequate
   B   produced
   C   misspent
   D   particular

7. The letters in **etopil** can be rearranged to make a word meaning

   A   well-mannered
   B   a low soft sound
   C   to make an unpleasantly loud, sharp cry
   D   very bright in colour or light, or very clever

8. Which pair of words is closest in meaning?

   A   scientists   rangers
   B   molten   lava
   C   surface   shore
   D   frantically   anxiously

9. Which pair of words is most opposite in meaning?

   A   baggy   flared
   B   puzzled   brilliant
   C   master   maid
   D   aching   moan

10. Which word should replace the words in bold in the following sentence?

    When he talked to the students about bullying, Mr Davis spoke **not in a joking manner**.

    A   sighed
    B   frantically
    C   seriously
    D   sobbing

© MR STEGGELS ADVANCED INSTRUCTION PTY LTD

11. Choose the best word to complete the sentence

    _____ the terrible food, I still managed to enjoy camp.

    A   Waste
    B   Pouring
    C   Quite
    D   Despite

12. You will most likely see protected species in a

    A   gum tree
    B   marsh
    C   game park
    D   billabong

13. Which word means **to defeat an opponent**?

    A   overcome
    B   obey
    C   tramp
    D   transform

14. Choose the word that is most similar in meaning to **perhaps**

    A   urge
    B   possibly
    C   too
    D   quite

15. Which is the odd word out?

    A   beanie
    B   trousers
    C   jersey
    D   umbrella

© MR STEGGELS ADVANCED INSTRUCTION PTY LTD

16. Choose the word that best completes the sentence

    The hikers paused to look at the vast _____ stretching below the mountain.

    A   billabong
    B   crops
    C   marsh
    D   plains

17. The letters in **ncsraheb** can be rearranged to make a word meaning

    A   parts of a tree that grow out from the main trunk and have leaves, flowers, or fruit on them
    B   created something
    C   the ground near a lake, a river, or the sea that is always wet
    D   the top layer of something

18. Which pair of words is most opposite in meaning?

    A   crooked   sideways
    B   neat   ragged
    C   particular   example
    D   judge   suggest

19. Choose the best definition of the word **throughout**

    A   on purpose, intended to make something happen
    B   enough
    C   permanent, never ending
    D   in every part of a place or object

20. Which word should replace the words in bold in the following sentence?

    When she saw the chocolate cake, she had the **strong feeling** to eat it all.

    A   urge
    B   nerves
    C   confidence
    D   panic

Test 3

1. Which word means **the set of tools needed for a particular purpose**?

    A   assortment
    B   practice
    C   antennae
    D   equipment

2. Choose the best meaning of the word **blockbuster**

    A   full of exciting events
    B   an unusual, exciting trip or experience
    C   a book or film that is very successful
    D   hot liquid rock that comes out of the Earth through a volcano

3. Choose the word that is closest in meaning to **assortment**

    A   things
    B   group
    C   mixture
    D   kind

4. Choose the word that is most opposite in meaning to **action-packed**

    A   dull
    B   exciting
    C   isolated
    D   neat

5. Which is the odd word out?

    A   floundered
    B   carrier
    C   isolated
    D   shuddered

© MR STEGGELS ADVANCED INSTRUCTION PTY LTD

6. Choose the word that best completes the sentence

   A _____ of seals was swimming next to our boat.

   A   colony
   B   nest
   C   undercurrent
   D   network

7. The letters in **smilesis** can be rearranged to make a word meaning

   A   in a way that shows you are worried and nervous
   B   connected to
   C   imaginary or not real
   D   flying weapons that can travel a long distance

8. Which word should replace the words in bold in the following sentence?

   Mr Smith was very successful in business but he had many **people who hated him**.

   A   habits
   B   enemies
   C   elders
   D   tales

9. Choose the best word to complete the sentence

   It is not a common _____ in this country to tip the waiter.

   A   habits
   B   production
   C   thread
   D   practice

10. Which word should replace the words in bold in the following sentence?

    We **moved quickly with small, short steps** back to our house when we heard the siren.

    A   dawdled
    B   scurried
    C   tramped
    D   panic

11. Choose the best word to complete the sentence

There was a ban on junk food_____ during children's TV programs.

    A   examples
    B   production
    C   shoplifting
    D   advertising

12. Where would you most likely find a **nest**?

    A   gum tree
    B   marsh
    C   game park
    D   billabong

13. Which of the following has **antennae**?

    A   ape
    B   missile
    C   grouch
    D   lobster

14. Which is sometimes played on a **lawn**?

    A   tennis
    B   rugby
    C   boomerang
    D   none of the above

15. Which of the following is green, white or purple in colour?

    A   gum tree
    B   cabbage
    C   soot
    D   arteries

© MR STEGGELS ADVANCED INSTRUCTION PTY LTD

16. Choose the word that best completes the sentence

    He _____ during his speech because his flash cards were out of order.

    A   floundered
    B   flared
    C   puzzled
    D   shuddered

17. The letters in **rcrirae** can be rearranged to make a word meaning

    A   facts about a situation, person or event
    B   a person who employs a servant
    C   a person or thing that holds or transports something
    D   extremely tiring and difficult, needing great effort

18. Which pair of words is most opposite in meaning?

    A   media   production
    B   polar   Arctic
    C   moaned   flared
    D   recent   old-fashioned

19. Choose the best definition of the word **undercurrent**

    A   a narrow current of water strongest near the surface that pulls away from the shore
    B   a strong wish, especially one that is difficult to control
    C   into, at or across the space separating two things
    D   a current below the surface

20. Which word should replace the words in bold in the following sentence?

    Sarah felt **quite apart from others** when she moved to a country town after living in the city.

    A   overcome
    B   anxious
    C   isolated
    D   proud

© MR STEGGELS ADVANCED INSTRUCTION PTY LTD

Test 4

1. Which word means **someone who complains a lot or is often angry**?

    A   maid
    B   master
    C   grouch
    D   elder

2. Choose the best meaning of the word **folktale**

    A   TV, newspapers, radio etc. as a group
    B   a book or film that is very successful
    C   stories about imaginary events or people
    D   a traditional story that people of a particular group repeat among themselves

3. Choose the category to which the other words belong

    A   grains
    B   fruits
    C   vegetables
    D   crops

4. Which is black in colour?

    A   bronze
    B   soot
    C   waste
    D   boomerang

5. Which is the odd word out?

    A   sideways
    B   thread
    C   rip
    D   gum tree

© MR STEGGELS ADVANCED INSTRUCTION PTY LTD

6. Choose the word that best completes the sentence

   Scientists are studying _____ bears to see how far they roam when hunting.

   A   hydrogen
   B   Arctic
   C   polar
   D   surface

---

7. The letters in **sayidsew** can be rearranged to make a word meaning

   A   extremely tiring and difficult, needing great effort
   B   a shirt that is worn by a member of a sports team
   C   wasted money or time
   D   in a direction to the left or right, not forwards or backwards

---

8. Which word should replace the words in bold in the following sentence?

   Mike's friends dared him to **take goods illegally** from the store without paying.

   A   rip
   B   shoplift
   C   misspent
   D   none of the above

---

9. Choose the best word to complete the sentence

   I only had white _____ so I couldn't repair the hole in my blue shirt.

   A   fashion
   B   equipment
   C   thread
   D   jersey

---

10. Which word should replace the words in bold in the following sentence?

    As we sat around the campfire, my uncle told us scary **stories about imaginary events**.

    A   information
    B   tales
    C   mythical
    D   enemies

11. Choose the best word to complete the sentence

    The Aborignial elder gave us a lesson on how to throw a _____ correctly.

    A   boomerang
    B   handkerchief
    C   missile
    D   BMX

12. Which is a metal?

    A   hydrogen
    B   bronze
    C   molten
    D   missile

13. Which of the following would you most likely find at a beach?

    A   umbrella
    B   rip
    C   undercurrent
    D   any of the above

14. What is another name for a **gum tree**?

    A   eucalyptus
    B   branches
    C   marsh
    D   none of the above

15. Which of the following has no colour, taste or smell?

    A   medicine
    B   cabbage
    C   soot
    D   hydrogen

© MR STEGGELS ADVANCED INSTRUCTION PTY LTD

16. Choose the word that best completes the sentence

    I was totally exhausted after the _____ cross-country race.

    A   grueling
    B   revolting
    C   disaster
    D   ragged

17. The letters in **ogsabtae** can be rearranged to make a word meaning

    A   difficult to understand
    B   gave a penalty to
    C   the two lights on the front of a car used for driving at night
    D   none of the above

18. Choose the group to which the other words belong

    A   beanie
    B   trousers
    C   jersey
    D   fashion

19. Choose the word most opposite in meaning to **crooked**

    A   sideways
    B   bend
    C   straight
    D   line

20. Which word should replace the words in bold in the following sentence?

    The Tasmanian tiger is a species that is **no longer in existence**.

    A   grueling
    B   dangerous
    C   complex
    D   extinct

© MR STEGGELS ADVANCED INSTRUCTION PTY LTD

Test 5

1. Which word means **breathe out slowly and noisily, expressing tiredness**?

    A   breath
    B   moan
    C   sigh
    D   shudder

2. Choose the best meaning of the word **rangers**

    A   people whose job is to protect a forest or natural park
    B   people who employ servants
    C   experts who study or work in one of the sciences
    D   people who have magic powers in stories, or who performs tricks for entertainment

3. The **Internet** is

    A   a number of computers that are connected together
    B   facts about a situation, person or event
    C   the world-wide system of connected computers that allows people to share information
    D   a set of pages about a particular subject

4. Choose the category to which the other words belong

    A   rugby
    B   sport
    C   tennis
    D   BMX

5. Which is the odd word out?

    A   overcome
    B   obey
    C   dawdle
    D   cute

© MR STEGGELS ADVANCED INSTRUCTION PTY LTD

6. Choose the word that best completes the sentence

   People began _____ around the magician as he expertly juggled six clubs.

   A   welcoming
   B   crowding
   C   advertising
   D   grueling

7. The letters in **wokrent** can be rearranged to make a word meaning

   A   this one and not any other
   B   a number of computers that are connected together
   C   the skill of fighting without weapons to protect yourself
   D   a show put on for an audience

8. Which word should replace the words in bold in the following sentence?

   We saw **a show put on for an audience** of *Seussical the musical* in the holidays.

   A   an animated
   B   a disaster
   C   an example
   D   a production

9. Choose the best word to complete the sentence

   This painting is a very good _____ of my skill with watercolours.

   A   production
   B   assortment
   C   business
   D   example

10. Which word should replace the words in bold in the following sentence?

    We had a lovely picnic on the **land along the edge** of the lake.

    A   perch
    B   lawn
    C   undercurrent
    D   shore

© MR STEGGELS ADVANCED INSTRUCTION PTY LTD

11. Choose the best word to complete the sentence

   The internal _____ engine is used to power most vehicles.

   A   hydrogen
   B   supersonic
   C   missile
   D   combustion

12. Choose the category to which the other words belong

   A   newspapers
   B   media
   C   TV
   D   radio

13. Which word means **to decide right from wrong**?

   A   translate
   B   suggest
   C   transform
   D   none of the above

14. Which word is closest in meaning to **meant**?

   A   intended
   B   changed
   C   decided
   D   suggest

15. A **polite** child is not likely to be

   A   brilliant
   B   adequate
   C   cheeky
   D   welcoming

© MR STEGGELS ADVANCED INSTRUCTION PTY LTD

16. Choose the word that best completes the sentence

    The performance was going to be _____ live and sold on DVD.

    A   recorded
    B   animated
    C   connected
    D   none of the above

17. The letters in **gghnniilt** can be rearranged to make a word meaning

    A   a hat made from wool with a small round wool ball on top
    B   the two lights on the front of a car used for driving at night
    C   likely to harm or kill someone, or to damage or destroy something
    D   light produced by electricity moving between clouds or from clouds to the ground

18. A film about a series of thrilling events is most likely to be

    A   mythical
    B   action-packed
    C   a blockbuster
    D   animated

19. Choose the word most opposite in meaning to **particular**

    A   isolated
    B   general
    C   waste
    D   complex

20. Which word means **a regular custom that is sometimes hard to give up**?

    A   practice
    B   urge
    C   habit
    D   business

© MR STEGGELS ADVANCED INSTRUCTION PTY LTD

Solutions

Unit 1

Definitions

1	trudged	5	breath	9	gum tree	13	scientists
2	frantically	6	marsh	10	Arctic	14	lava
3	surface	7	polar	11	pouring	15	sobbing
4	nest	8	branches	12	equipment	16	tennis

Word usage

1	scientists	5	frantically	9	marsh	13	Arctic
2	pouring	6	breath	10	Polar	14	branches
3	equipment	7	trudged	11	surface	15	nest
4	lava	8	sobbing	12	gum tree	16	tennis

Unit 2

Definitions

1	sideways	5	produced	9	adventure	13	rangers
2	blockbuster	6	shuddered	10	misspent	14	game park
3	action-packed	7	despite	11	practice	15	forehead
4	floundered	8	crooked	12	crops	16	enemies

Word usage

1	rangers	5	produced	9	adventure	13	shuddered
2	crops	6	action-packed	10	despite	14	forehead
3	misspent	7	blockbuster	11	enemies	15	practice
4	game park	8	sideways	12	floundered	16	crooked

Unit 3

Definitions

1	old-fashioned	5	sabotage	9	billabong	13	website
2	maid	6	network	10	carrier	14	Internet
3	plains	7	master	11	connected	15	grueling
4	elders	8	information	12	jersey	16	soot

Unit 3

Word usage

1	website	5	plains	9	billabong	13	old-fashioned
2	jersey	6	master	10	elders	14	information
3	Internet	7	connected	11	carrier	15	network
4	grueling	8	maid	12	sabotage	16	soot

Unit 4

Definitions

1	beanie	5	grouch	9	nerves	13	animated
2	revolting	6	squash	10	dangerous	14	production
3	lightning	7	headlights	11	computer	15	umbrella
4	tales	8	neighbourhood	12	punished	16	complex

Word usage

1	tales	5	beanie	9	dangerous	13	production
2	neighbourhood	6	punished	10	umbrella	14	animated
3	grouch	7	headlights	11	revolting	15	computer
4	nerves	8	lightning	12	complex	16	squash

Unit 5

Definitions

1	extinct	5	self-defence	9	spiritual	13	habits
2	particular	6	mythical	10	health	14	arteries
3	overcome	7	veins	11	recorded	15	illness
4	linked	8	isolated	12	waste	16	medicine

Word usage

1	medicine	5	particular	9	arteries	13	linked
2	illness	6	mythical	10	spiritual	14	waste
3	habits	7	veins	11	self-defence	15	extinct
4	health	8	isolated	12	overcome	16	recorded

© MR STEGGELS ADVANCED INSTRUCTION PTY LTD

Unit 6

Definitions

1	too	5	shoplift	9	advertising	13	quite
2	lawn	6	gleefully	10	undercurrent	14	missiles
3	anxiously	7	between	11	urge	15	rip
4	aching	8	puzzled	12	obey	16	BMX

Word usage

1	BMX	5	puzzled	9	too	13	gleefully
2	rip	6	aching	10	anxiously	14	quite
3	shoplift	7	obey	11	lawn	15	between
4	advertising	8	missiles	12	urge	16	undercurrent

Unit 7

Definitions

1	fashion	5	bronze	9	neat	13	baggy
2	furious	6	apes	10	disaster	14	business
3	cute	7	tramp	11	proud	15	dawdle
4	moaned	8	clump	12	flared	16	thread

Word usage

1	baggy	5	bronze	9	moaned	13	disaster
2	business	6	apes	10	thread	14	tramp
3	cute	7	proud	11	clump	15	neat
4	dawdle	8	flared	12	furious	16	fashion

Unit 8

Definitions

1	rugby	5	crowding	9	hopeful	13	reporter
2	antennae	6	barn	10	possibly	14	example
3	satisfied	7	scurried	11	trousers	15	colony
4	ragged	8	confidence	12	boomerang	16	folktale

Unit 8

Word usage

1	boomerang	5	antennae	9	folktale	13	colony
2	trousers	6	barn	10	hopeful	14	crowding
3	reporter	7	scurried	11	ragged	15	possibly
4	example	8	confidence	12	satisfied	16	rugby

Unit 9

Definitions

1	judge	5	meant	9	adequate	13	transform
2	media	6	brilliant	10	suggest	14	throughout
3	polite	7	welcoming	11	panic	15	everlasting
4	translate	8	seriously	12	temporary	16	assortment

Word usage

1	brilliant	5	everlasting	9	translate	13	polite
2	judge	6	assortment	10	media	14	throughout
3	transform	7	suggest	11	welcoming	15	meant
4	adequate	8	temporary	12	seriously	16	panic

Unit 10

Definitions

1	shore	5	overhanging	9	naughtiest	13	combustion
2	cheeky	6	sighed	10	hydrogen	14	cabbage
3	hospital	7	perched	11	professor	15	supersonic
4	cooed	8	handkerchief	12	magician	16	squawk

Word usage

1	cheeky	5	hydrogen	9	handkerchief	13	cabbage
2	perched	6	cooed	10	hospital	14	combustion
3	overhanging	7	naughtiest	11	professor	15	supersonic
4	shore	8	sighed	12	squawk	16	magician

© MR STEGGELS ADVANCED INSTRUCTION PTY LTD

Test 1 solutions

Q	A	Notes
1	D	**pouring** means flowing quickly and in large amounts
2	C	an **adventure** is an unusual, exciting trip or experience
3	A	to **wreck** something is to **sabotage** it
4	D	the opposite of **rewarded** is **punished**
5	D	A, B and C are parts of the body
6	B	To learn about lions, I searched for **information** on the Internet.
7	A	delser → **elders** older people especially with respected positions in society
8	D	**connected** and **linked** both mean joined
9	C	**temporary** is for a short time; **everlasting** is forever
10	C	The criminal had to **transform** his appearance to avoid being captured.
11	C	the opposite of spent is **misspent**
12	B	**BMX** stands for bicycle motocross
13	A	**quite** means to a certain degree → I was **quite** certain that I would pass the test.
14	B	**confused** and **puzzled** both mean unable to understand
15	D	A, B and C are occupations/jobs
16	C	Martial arts is a form of **self-defence**.
17	A	ginahc → **aching** continuous unpleasant pain
18	A	**tramp** and **dawdle** both mean to walk slowly
19	B	a **computer** is an electronic device that stores information and runs programs
20	C	The questions in the test were too **complex** for students in the first grade.

© MR STEGGELS ADVANCED INSTRUCTION PTY LTD

Test 2 solutions

Q	A	Notes
1	A	**squawk** means to make an unpleasantly loud, sharp cry
2	D	**perched** means sat on or near the edge of something, especially a bird
3	D	**contented** and **satisfied** are similar in meaning
4	C	**illness** is the opposite to good **health**
5	C	A, B and D are adverbs (ending in –ly); **hopeful** is an adjective
6	A	On our zoo excursion, we had **adequate** time to see all of the animals.
7	A	etopil → **polite** well-mannered
8	D	**frantically** and **anxiously** both involve panic/worry
9	C	**master** is opposite to servant (**maid**)
10	C	When he talked to the students about bullying, Mr Davis spoke **seriously**.
11	D	**Despite** the terrible food, I still managed to enjoy camp.
12	C	a **game park** is an area of land set aside to protect wild animals
13	A	**overcome** means to defeat an opponent
14	B	**perhaps** and **possibly** both mean maybe
15	D	A, B and C are items of clothing
16	D	The hikers paused to look at the vast **plains** stretching below the mountain.
17	A	ncsraheb → **branches** parts of a tree that grow out from the main trunk and have leaves, flowers, or fruit on them
18	B	**neat** and **ragged** are opposites
19	D	**throughout** means in every part of a place or object
20	A	When she saw the chocolate cake, she had the **urge** to eat it all.

© MR STEGGELS ADVANCED INSTRUCTION PTY LTD

Test 3 solutions

Q	A	Notes
1	D	**equipment** means the set of tools needed for a particular purpose
2	C	**blockbuster** means a book or film that is very successful
3	C	an **assortment** is a mixture
4	A	**action-packed** is the opposite to **dull**
5	B	A, B and D are verbs ending in –ed; **carrier** is a noun
6	A	A **colony** of seals was swimming next to our boat.
7	D	**smilesis → missiles** flying weapons that can travel a long distance
8	B	Mr Smith was very successful in business but he had many **enemies**.
9	D	It is not a common **practice** in this country to tip the waiter.
10	B	We **scurried** back to our house when we heard the siren.
11	D	There was a ban on junk food **advertising** during children's TV programs.
12	A	a **nest** a structure built by birds or insects to leave their eggs in; birds live in trees
13	D	**antennae** are a pair of long, thin organs that are found on the heads of insects and crustaceans; a lobster is a crustacean
14	A	**tennis** is played on **lawn** (grass)
15	B	**cabbage** is a large round vegetable with green, white, or purple leaves that can be eaten cooked or uncooked
16	A	He **floundered** during his speech because his flash cards were out of order.
17	C	**rcrirae → carrier** a person or thing that holds or transports something
18	D	**recent** and **old-fashioned** are opposites
19	D	an **undercurrent** is a current below the surface
20	C	Sarah felt **isolated** when she moved to a country town after living in the city.

© MR STEGGELS ADVANCED INSTRUCTION PTY LTD

Test 4 solutions

Q	A	Notes
1	C	a **grouch** is someone who complains a lot or is often angry
2	D	a **folktale** is a traditional story that people of a particular group repeat among themselves
3	D	grains, fruits and vegetables are all **crops**
4	B	**soot** is black in colour
5	A	B, C and D are nouns; **sideways** is an adjective
6	C	Scientists are studying **polar** bears to see how far they roam when hunting.
7	D	**sayidsew** → **sidways** in a direction to the left or right, not forwards or backwards
8	B	Mike's friends dared him to **shoplift** from the store without paying.
9	C	I only had white **thread** so I couldn't repair the hole in my blue shirt.
10	B	As we sat around the campfire, my uncle told us scary **tales**.
11	A	The Aboriginal elder gave us a lesson on how to throw a **boomerang** correctly.
12	B	**bronze** is a brown metal made of copper and tin
13	D	you would find and **umbrella**, a **rip** and an **undercurrent** at a beach
14	A	a **gum tree** is also known as a **eucalyptus** tree
15	D	**hydrogen** is the lightest gas, with no colour, taste, or smell, and combines with oxygen to form water
16	A	I was totally exhausted after the **grueling** cross-country race.
17	D	**ogsabtae** → **sabotage** to destroy equipment, weapons, or buildings on purpose
18	D	a **beanie**, a **jersey** and a pair of **trousers** are **fashion**
19	C	**crooked** and **straight** are opposites
20	D	The Tasmanian tiger is a species that is **extinct**.

Test 5 solutions

Q	A	Notes
1	C	**sigh** means to breathe out slowly and noisily, expressing tiredness
2	A	**rangers** are people whose job is to protect a forest or natural park
3	C	The **Internet** is the world-wide system of connected computers that allows people to share information
4	B	A, C and D are sports
5	D	A, B and C are verbs; **cute** is an adjective
6	B	People began **crowding** around the magician as he juggled six clubs.
7	B	**wokrent → network** a number of computers that are connected together
8	D	We saw **a production** of *Seussical the musical* in the holidays.
9	D	This painting is a very good **example** of my skill with watercolours.
10	D	We had a lovely picnic on the **shore** of the lake.
11	D	The internal **combustion** engine is used to power most vehicles.
12	B	A, C and D are examples of **media**
13	D	**judge** means to decide right from wrong
14	A	**meant** and **intended** are similar in meaning
15	C	a **polite** child is well-mannered; a **cheeky** child is rude in a humorous way
16	A	The performance was going to be **recorded** live and sold on DVD.
17	D	**gghnniilt → lightning** is light produced by electricity moving between clouds or from clouds to the ground
18	B	A film about a series of thrilling events is most likely to be **action-packed**.
19	B	**particular** and **general** are opposites
20	C	a **habit** is a regular custom that is sometimes hard to give up.

© MR STEGGELS ADVANCED INSTRUCTION PTY LTD

www.ingramcontent.com/pod-product-compliance
Lightning Source LLC
LaVergne TN
LVHW061318060426
835507LV00019B/2213